MAN OF VALOR

31 DAY DEVOTIONAL

MAN OF VALOR

31 DAY DEVOTIONAL

by DeAngela S. Reid
© 2019

Copyright © 2019
by DeAngela S. Reid

All rights reserved. No part of this book may be reprinted or reproduced in any form or by any electronic, mechanical, or other means, now known or hereafter invented, including photocopy, recording, and information storage and retrieval, without permission in writing from the publisher.

ISBN: 978-0-9996746-7-3
Library of Congress Control Number: 2019907422

Designed & Published by:
The Solid Foundation Group, LLC
Atlanta, Georgia
www.TheSolidFoundationGroup.com

Cover Designed by:
Amber Totten, Freshwind Graphics

Printed in the United States of America

In loving memory of Bishop Gary Bernard Jones

INTRODUCTION

Man of Valor was written specifically with men in mind. Helping them to spend intimate time with God and become men after God's own heart. It also deals with practical issues that we all face in life.

A Poetry Moment…

MAN OF VALOR

Clothed in honor and strength,
he is equipped to defend
what is his as well as what is right.
Although, he may be facing danger
he doesn't run from the fight
because he has learned to
walk by faith and not by sight.
Many see him as brave
and even a hero of sorts
simply because he walks in integrity
and truth any given day.
Far from perfect but he is a
man of valor in every single way.

TABLE OF CONTENTS

ALPHA & OMEGA	1
TEMPTATION	2
IDENTITY CRISIS	3
AVOIDING PRIDE	4
A BREAK FROM IT ALL	5
BE YE READY	6
A WORK OF ART	7
TEACHING GENERATIONS	8
IN HIS PRESENCE	9
REAL MEN PRAISE GOD	10
WISDOM FOR THE TAKING	11

THE LORD WILL DO THE LIFTING	12
HUNGRY FOR THE WORD	13
ASSEMBLY & FELLOWSHIP	14
PRIME EXAMPLE	15
HIS GRACE IS SUFFICIENT	16
SURRENDERING TO GOD	17
START THINKING STRAIGHT	18
GET YOUR MIND RIGHT	19
FORGIVE AND LET GO	20
WE ARE CALLED TO WORK	21
NO BLESSING ZONE	22
FORGE AHEAD	23
HE'S A REWARDER	24
STAYING SHARP	25
LOVE IS AN ACTION WORD	26
REAL STRENGTH	27
BE DILIGENT	28
HERO	29
IT'S CALLED SACRIFICE	30
PRAYING POWER	31

DAY 1

"Everything Starts and Ends with God"
THE ALPHA & OMEGA

Revelation 22:13 (KJV)
I am Alpha and Omega, the beginning and the end, the first and the last.

Recognizing that God was in the beginning of all things and that He will be there in the closing kinda puts things into perspective. In scripture, He is not simply referring to the beginning and ending of the Greek alphabet but He is the absolute first and the absolute conclusion. What does that mean for us? He is eternal, so in essence Jesus is all we need from here to eternity.

Today's Sentence Prayer
Dear Lord, please help me remain mindful that you are party to everything concerning my life because you are the Alpha and Omega. In the precious name of Jesus, I pray… Amen.

"Escaping the Forbidden Fruit"
TEMPTATION

1 Corinthians 10:13 (KJV)
There hath no temptation taken you but such as is common to man: God is faithful, who will not suffer you to be tempted above that ye are able; but will temptation also make a way to escape, that ye may be able to bear it.

Quite candidly, we are mere humans which means we all face temptation of some sort. The temptations may vary from individual to individual but we all have them. We can take comfort in the fact that our Heavenly father has assured us a way of escape.

Today's Sentence Prayer
Dear Lord, please help me as I fight with my various temptations in life as they are impossible to fight in my own strength. In Jesus' name, I pray...Amen.

"Knowing Whose You Are"
IDENTITY CRISIS

1 Peter 2:9 (KJV)
9 But ye are a chosen generation, a royal priesthood, a holy nation, a peculiar people; that ye should shew forth the praises of him who hath called you out of darkness into his marvellous light;

Often times we live beneath our privilege and settle for many things in this journey called life all because we don't recognize our true identity...our identity in Christ along with all of its many remarkable benefits.

Today's Sentence Prayer
Dear Lord, please help me to always be aware of who and whose I am in this life so I won't ever settle for less than your best for me. In Jesus' name, I pray...Amen.

"Before the Fall"
AVOIDING PRIDE

Proverbs 16:18 (KJV)
Pride goeth before destruction, and an haughty spirit before a fall.

We should always be most gracious avoiding conceit and arrogance. Recognize that confidence and arrogance are not one in the same. Always consider others and learn to lighten up and laugh at yourself. The world can and will keep revolving with or without you.

Today's Sentence Prayer
Dear Lord, please develop in me a genuine spirit of humility so that I will not think more of myself than I ought. In Jesus' name, I pray…Amen.

"Learning To Relax And Rest"
A BREAK FROM IT ALL

Mark 6:31 (KJV)
31 And he said unto them, Come ye yourselves apart into a desert place, and rest a while: for there were many coming and going, and they had no leisure so much as to eat.

Rest is a necessity and if you don't come apart then you will come apart. Even Almighty God took time for rest so surely we know how important is that we do the same. You should indeed make it a priority.

Today's Sentence Prayer
Dear Lord, please help me to break away from being a workaholic so that I can learn to relax and rest for my overall health and well-being. In Jesus' name, I pray...Amen.

"Grounded In Your Beliefs"
BE YE READY

1 Peter 3:15 (KJV)
But sanctify the Lord God in your hearts: and be ready always to give an answer to every man that asketh you a reason of the hope that is in you with meekness and fear

---

We as Christians should be prepared to witness at any given moment to hearts prepared to receive our Lord and Savior Jesus Christ. Have you studied the word? Are you ready right now?

Today's Sentence Prayer
Dear Lord, bless me to be an excellent student of your word preparing me to witness at any time and may my lifestyle witness louder and clearer than any words every could. In Jesus' name, I pray…Amen.

DAY 7

"God's Workmanship"
A WORK OF ART

Ephesians 2:10 (KJV)
10 For we are his workmanship, created in Christ Jesus unto good works, which God hath before ordained that we should walk in them.

God Himself put so much detail into not only making us but making each of us unique. We are all His masterpiece…a true work of art.

Today's Sentence Prayer
Dear Lord, may I always recognize my value since you put so much effort in creating me with my uniqueness. In Jesus' name, I pray…Amen.

"Leaving A Spiritual Legacy"
TEACHING GENERATIONS

Psalm 78:4 (KJV)
4 We will not hide them from their children, shewing to the generation to come the praises of the Lord, and his strength, and his wonderful works that he hath done.

God desires us to teach our children of His person, His ways, and His statutes so that our children will teach their children and so forth. This legacy is actually more rich than silver or gold.

Today's Sentence Prayer
Dear Lord, please help me study to show myself approved so that many generations to come will be richly rewarded with this spiritual legacy. In Jesus' name, I pray…Amen.

"Fullness of Joy"
IN HIS PRESENCE

Psalm 16:11 (KJV)
Thou wilt shew me the path of life: in thy presence is fulness of joy; at thy right hand there are pleasures for evermore.

There is absolutely no place like the presence of God. This place brings about peace of mind and clarity. It is where everyone should start the decision-making process because God cares about the affairs of your life.

Today's Sentence Prayer
Dear Lord, please help me deliberately clear my schedule to make time to meet you in our secret place so that I can start my day correctly. In Jesus' name I pray…Amen.

"Speak Up and Let The World Know"
REAL MEN PRAISE GOD

Psalm 107:2 (KJV)
Let the redeemed of the Lord say so, whom he hath redeemed from the hand of the enemy

---

God's word says let the redeemed of the Lord say so. God is not looking for any secret service agents for the kingdom. You should never feel too cool, macho or haughty that you can't give God some praise. He's been too good to keep it to yourself.

Today's Sentence Prayer
Dear Lord, may the words of my mouth and meditation of my heart be acceptable in your sight and may my demonstrative praise be a pleasing fragrance to your nostrils. In Jesus' name, I pray...Amen.

DAY 11

"You Can Have It If You Ask"
WISDOM FOR THE TAKING

James 1:5 (KJV)
If any of you lack wisdom, let him ask of God, that giveth to all men liberally, and upbraideth not; and it shall be given him.

If you lack wisdom, ask God and He will generously give it to you. It is God's desire that you operate daily in godly wisdom so that your way will be made prosperous.

Today's Sentence Prayer
Dear Lord, please give me godly wisdom that I can apply to my life daily. In Jesus's name, I pray...Amen.

"Please Be Humble"
THE LORD WILL DO THE LIFTING

James 4:10 (KJV)
Humble yourselves in the sight of the Lord, and he shall lift you up.

If you will humble yourself then God Himself will exalt you in due season and He will make your name great. God takes pleasure in blessing His children greatly so remain humble so that He can bless you the way that He desires.

Today's Sentence Prayer
Dear Lord, please help me to remain humble in all situations in life. In Jesus' name, I pray…Amen.

"Going Full Speed Ahead"
HUNGRY FOR THE WORD

Matthew 5:6 (KJV)
Blessed are they which do hunger and thirst after righteousness: for they shall be filled.

We should have a hunger and thirst for God's word and righteousness for it is truly what gives us life. It's our manual for how to live this life we've been given and for how to manage God's affairs and belongings that He has entrusted to us to oversee.

Today's Sentence Prayer
Dear Lord, please help me to consistently study your mighty and matchless word that guides and blesses my life.   In Jesus' name, I pray...Amen.

DAY 14

"Church is Important"
ASSEMBLY & FELLOWSHIP

Hebrews 10:25 (KJV)
Not forsaking the assembling of ourselves together, as the manner of some is; but exhorting one another: and so much the more, as ye see the day approaching.

It's important to God and for us that we not only attend church regularly but also be active members of our church communities then we can accomplish His goals.

Today's Sentence Prayer
Dear Lord, please align me in the right spiritual location to receive the messages you have regarding my life. In Jesus' name, I pray…Amen.

"He Paved The Way"
PRIME EXAMPLE

Philippians 2:5-8 (KJV)
5 Let this mind be in you, which was also in Christ Jesus: 6 Who, being in the form of God, thought it not robbery to be equal with God: 7 But made himself of no reputation, and took upon him the form of a servant, and was made in the likeness of men:8 And being found in fashion as a man, he humbled himself, and became obedient unto death, even the death of the cross.

As Christians, we are representatives for the kingdom of God. We are by no means perfect and we are not expected to be great representatives within our own strength but rather with the power of the Holy Spirit. People are watching your life to see the works of this Mighty God you serve.

Today's Sentence Prayer
Dear Lord, please help me to consistency follow the very example that you have set before me. In Jesus' name, I pray...Amen.

"May Seem Tough But He Won't Remove The Thorn"
HIS GRACE IS SUFFICIENT

2 Corinthians 12:9 (KJV)
And he said unto me, My grace is sufficient for thee: for my strength is made perfect in weakness. Most gladly therefore will I rather glory in my infirmities, that the power of Christ may rest upon me.

We often experience some painful things in this journey that we call life. God won't always remove us from those situations because they were designed for our growth and development but He will extend His grace to help up cope with our experiences.

Today's Sentence Prayer
Dear Lord, speak to my heart and hear my cry unto you and if this is not the day that my circumstances to change grant me coping grace to get through my trials. In Jesus' name, I pray…Amen.

"We Are Not In Control"
SURRENDERING TO GOD

Isaiah 45:9 (KJV)
Woe unto him that striveth with his Maker! Let the potsherd strive with the potsherds of the earth. Shall the clay say to him that fashioneth it, What makest thou? or thy work, He hath no hands?

Many of us struggle with control issues because we hate depending on other people but the truth of the matter is that we are really not in control of own affairs anyway. Surrendering to God requires that we have a reality check and recognize who is really in control.

Today's Sentence Prayer
Dear Lord, please help me put things into perspective and see that you are indeed in total control. In Jesus' name, I pray...Amen.

"Called to Be Sober Minded"
START THINKING STRAIGHT

Romans 12:3 (KJV)
3 For I say, through the grace given unto me, to every man that is among you, not to think of himself more highly than he ought to think; but to think soberly, according as God hath dealt to every man the measure of faith.

Ephesians 5:18 (KJV)
18 And be not drunk with wine, wherein is excess; but be filled with the Spirit.

God requires us to think soberly because we are His ambassadors which means we have work to do on this side of heaven. We can't afford to waste time with stinking thinking.

Today's Sentence Prayer
Dear Lord, I pray that you will help me get and keep my mind right so that I will live a life pleasing unto you. It is in Jesus' name, I pray...Amen.

"Mind Makeover…Renew Your Mind"
GET YOUR MIND RIGHT

Romans 12:2 (KJV)
And be not conformed to this world: but be ye transformed by the renewing of your mind, that ye may prove what is that good, and acceptable, and perfect, will of God.

According to the word of God we need a mental overhaul. Time to trade in our worldly wisdom and seek to know and do God's will.

Today's Sentence Prayer
Dear Lord, please help me to renew my mind so that my life is not governed by the ways of the world but rather by your holy word. In Jesus' name, I pray…Amen.

"Putting Resentment Behind Us"
FORGIVE AND LET IT GO

Mark 11:25 (KJV)
And when ye stand praying, forgive, if ye have ought against any: that your Father also which is in heaven may forgive you your trespasses.

You must realize that forgiveness is for your healing not for the person that you need to forgive, because grudges weigh you down and keep your heart burdened. So, free yourself and please release that. Learn to forgive yourself too because God already has done so.

Today's Sentence Prayer
Dear Lord, please help release the burden of unforgiveness so that I can forgive everyone that I feel has wronged me in some way. In Jesus' name, I pray…Amen.

"Used by God...Real Ambassadors"
WE ARE CALLED TO WORK

2 Corinthians 5:20 (KJV)
Now then we are ambassadors for Christ, as though God did beseech you by us: we pray you in Christ's stead, be ye reconciled to God.

We are called to represent God's kingdom and to work with and for God in the earth realm. We must take our responsibility seriously as we strive to live a life pleasing unto our King.

Today's Sentence Prayer
Dear Lord, please help me to represent your kingdom in absolute excellence. In Jesus' name, I pray...Amen.

"No Duplicity nor Double-Mindedness"
NO BLESSING ZONE

James 1:8 (KJV)
A double minded man is unstable in all his ways.

The word of God says that a double-minded man can't be blessed and that God will spit out those that are lukewarm. Pick your team and play consistently.

Today's Sentence Prayer
Dear Lord, please help to always know what I stand for and why I stand for it, so that I am never wishy-washy or unstable. In Jesus' name, I pray…Amen.

"New Beginnings"
FORGE AHEAD

Philippians 3:13 (KJV)
Brethren, I count not myself to have apprehended: but this one thing I do, forgetting those things which are behind, and reaching forth unto those things which are before,

---

Moving forward requires day-by-day faith and growing in His word. We cannot afford to be spiritually or emotionally paralyzed, because God has work for us to do as we dwell here on earth. Relinquish the past, embrace the present and keep moving forward toward the future.

Today's Sentence Prayer
Dear Lord, please help me to let go of my past so that I can keep pressing my way towards my blessed future. In Jesus' name, I pray…Amen.

"Diligently Seeking"
HE'S A REWARDER

Hebrews 11:6 (KJV)
But without faith it is impossible to please him: for he that cometh to God must believe that he is, and that he is a rewarder of them that diligently seek him.

God is not like man, He cannot lie and it's clearly stated that He is a rewarder of those that diligently seek Him and His righteousness. What are you truly seeking? Do you want His rewards?

Today's Sentence Prayer
Dear Lord, please help me avoid destructions and pitfalls that would seek to hinder me from consistently studying your word. In Jesus' name, I pray…Amen.

"Accountability Partners"
STAYING SHARP

Proverbs 27:17 (KJV)
Iron sharpeneth iron; so a man sharpeneth
the countenance of his friend.

There is wisdom found in godly counsel as well as having someone to help hold you accountable in this life for your words, thoughts and deeds. Ask God to send those people to the forefront of your life so that you can live the best life possible.

Today's Sentence Prayer
Dear Lord, please send god-fearing individuals into my life to hold me accountable. In Jesus' name, I pray…Amen.

"It's Not Just Something That You Say"
LOVE IS AN ACTION WORD

1 Corinthians 13:4-8
4 Charity suffereth long, and is kind; charity envieth not; charity vaunteth not itself, is not puffed up,5 Doth not behave itself unseemly, seeketh not her own, is not easily provoked, thinketh no evil;6 Rejoiceth not in iniquity, but rejoiceth in the truth;7 Beareth all things, believeth all things, hopeth all things, endureth all things.8 Charity never faileth: but whether there be prophecies, they shall fail; whether there be tongues, they shall cease; whether there be knowledge, it shall vanish away ((KJV))

It means absolutely nothing to say that you have love in your heart but you treat people horribly. The love of God residing within you should not be a major secret, let the world in on it.

Today's Sentence Prayer
Dear Lord, please grant me the ability to share your love for the world with the people of the world. In Jesus' name, I pray... Amen.

"Where It Comes From"
REAL STRENGTH

Philippians 4:13 (KJV)
I can do all things through Christ which strengtheneth me.

It's important to recognize where real strength comes from, because it's not something that we can bestow upon ourselves but rather it's something that comes from our savior helping us to accomplish the tasks at hand.

Today's Sentence Prayer
Dear Lord, please help me to not attempt to rely on my own strength to accomplish my goals and duties but to rely upon you. In Jesus' name, I pray...Amen.

"Lazy Costs Entirely Too Much"
BE DILIGENT

Proverbs 10:4-5 (KJV)
4 He becometh poor that dealeth with a slack hand: but the hand of the diligent maketh rich. 5 He that gathereth in summer is a wise son: but he that sleepeth in harvest is a son that causeth shame.

Laziness is a trap designed to make you miss your blessings and destiny. Do your part in life and watch God put His Super on your natural.

Today's Sentence Prayer
Dear Lord, please help me avoid laziness at all cost so that it won't cost me everything. In Jesus' name, I pray…Amen.

"There Are People Depending On The Warrior In You"
HERO

Judges 6:12 (KJV)
And the angel of the Lord appeared unto him, and said unto him, The Lord is with thee, thou mighty man of valour.

People need you to step up to be the man that God created you to be. The will of God is the best and safest place to be, and in this place you will be led by God as others are following you.

Today's Sentence Prayer
Dear Lord, please give me the strength to make it through the storms of my life because there are people depending on the warrior within me. In Jesus' name, I pray…Amen.

"Sometimes You Have To Forgo"
IT'S CALLED SACRIFICE

John 3:16 (KJV)
For God so loved the world, that he gave his only begotten Son, that whosoever believeth in him should not perish, but have everlasting life.

Sacrifice is not always an easy thing to do, because often times it could be quite uncomfortable. God sacrificed His son for us, because of His love for us, which is a prime example of what love and sacrifice look like.

Today's Sentence Prayer
Dear Lord, please grant me the ability to make necessary sacrifices along this journey that we call life. In Jesus' name, I pray…Amen.

"Prayer Works Indeed"
PRAYING POWER

James 5:16 (KJV)
Confess your faults one to another, and pray one for another, that ye may be healed. The effectual fervent prayer of a righteous man availeth much.

Prayer has the power to change circumstances, people, outlooks and much more in life. It is a powerful tool that God has equipped us with but it is up to you to use the tool. It is not about you forming the perfect words but rather humbling yourself and having a genuine conversation with God, so tap into that power.

Today's Sentence Prayer
Dear Lord, please help me to consistently bring all issues and concerns of life to you in prayer. In Jesus' name, I pray…Amen.

THE SOLID FOUNDATION GROUP

Other Books to Enjoy:
www.TheSolidFoundationGroup.com

Man of Valor – 31 Day Devotional
by DeAngela S. Reid

Genre: Religion / Spirituality

Bountiful Blessings – 31 Day Devotional
by DeAngela S. Reid

Genre: Religion / Spirituality

Pieces of Her Life
by G.C. Tindley

Genre: Fiction / Erotic Fiction

Live Every Moment
by Shatanese Reese

Genre: Autobiography / Inspirational

Bullet Proof
by Bodie Quinette

Genre: Christian Non-Fiction / Self-Help

A Portrait of Virginia A. Smith
by Virginia A. Smith

Genre: Memoire / Inspirational

Poetic Motifs' Significance of 9
by Kish Andes

Genre: Poetry

How To Fade Like Griffin
by Kendrick Henderson

Genre: Trade / Educational

The Pig Who Became President
By Alana Johnson

Genre: Children's

Set Free by Truth
By Amari Johnson

Genre: Children's / Science Fiction

CheckMate
by Lex

Genre: Urban

The Cartel's Daughter Unedited
by Carmine

Genre: Urban

All are Available in Paperback or E-Book Formats

Anywhere Books Are Sold*

amazon BARNES &NOBLE   Google Play BAM! BOOKS-A-MILLION

Your online review for any of the listed books will be greatly appreciated.

To learn more about the authors and/ or their upcoming books [or] to obtain information about becoming an author yourself, please visit our website:

www.TheSolidFoundationGroup.com

www.ingramcontent.com/pod-product-compliance
Lightning Source LLC
Chambersburg PA
CBHW070739020526
44118CB00035B/1757